DIGRESSIONS OF A NAKED PARTY GIRL

Sky Gilbert

DIGRESSIONS OF A NAKED PARTY GIRL

ECW PRESS

The publication of *Digressions of a Naked Party Girl* has been generously supported by The Canada Council, the Ontario Arts Council, and the Government of Canada through the Book Publishing Industry Development Program.

CANADIAN CATALOGUING IN PUBLICATION DATA

Gilbert, Sky 1952–
Digressions of a naked party girl

Poems.
ISBN 1-55022-364-X

I. Title.

PS8563.14743D53 1998   C811'.54   C98-931403-0
PR9199.3.G54D53 1998

Edited for the press by Michael Holmes.

Imaging by ECW Type & Art, Oakville, Ontario.
Printed by Marc Veilleux Imprimeur, Boucherville, Québec.

Distributed in Canada by General Distribution Services, 325 Humber College Blvd., Etobicoke, Ontario M9W 7C3.

Published by ECW PRESS,
2120 Queen Street East, Suite 200,
Toronto, Ontario M4E 1E2.

www.ecw.ca/press

TABLE OF CONTENTS

ODE TO PRESIDENT WILLIAM JEFFERSON CLINTON

I never thought I'd be writing an ode to you
after all those Big Macs
But it's just before nine o'clock on January 27, 1998
and I gave up nude swimming
just to hear your State of the Union address
(I didn't really want to go anyway)
I hope you're lying
I hope you did have sex with them all, every single girl
with big teeth and big hair
The same as every mother in America, I look at you
quite differently now
Now you're a pervert, like me
And there are all sorts of wonderful homosexual things
about you like
a) your arrangement with your wife
b) the fact that you think oral sex isn't adultery, and
c) that you don't look fifty
O send those girls to Washington
In the past, they might just have become dry Republican
husks of women,
withering like William Inge schoolteachers, on the steps
of the Lincoln Memorial
Instead they run to you, hair uncombed by a summer
breeze, having forgotten to wear underwear to that
particular White House event
Just remember Judy Holliday was fucking Bill Holden,
in *Born Yesterday*,
and that was much more important than wearing glasses
and learning The Declaration of Independence
No, it was some sort of declaration

And Monica Lewinsky was an ugly fat girl
until just a few months *before* she fucked a president
and discovered (somehow, on her own) that she was free,
white trash, and twenty-one
To some it's exploitation and depravity
And me, well I will never forget the moment when, at
some public function, you swept her into your arms and
she was all breathless and horny
like some young man
You see where it all connects
It's all about a kind of expectation, that sometimes
encompasses uncertainty and a kind of difficulty in not
touching that which is offered, in admiration
and bewilderment and danger and urgency and fear
And love

REFLECTIONS ON JUDY

for Nick

Of course I was very stoned and there were lots of campy
guys and cruising guys standing around but
There she was
(end of *Mrs. Dalloway*, literary reference, some sort of
image of feminine ascendancy meaning everything
feminine or the essence of of of)
Too many sparkles (can there ever be too many sparkles?)
And she knows HOW to wear that dress
(but daahhhhrling)
How many drugs is she on?
Which ones?
Yes long legs, but the dress is too tight
When she sits down we feel for her tummy
And the hair, a maniacal pageboy
And from certain angles she's in *Meet Me In St. Louis*
again
And Liza's only a baby
From other angles she's a hundred years old and Liza is
stiff competition
And why do we care?
Why do we care about this very wrecked lady, who is
almost as wrecked as we are?
Oh there she goes again
She's gone into some sort of frenzy, arms all akimbo
Is it because she's just like every desperate drunken horny
woman you've every met at parties only she has talent
(lots of it)?
What do she and Mick Jagger have in common?

Only we don't stand in a bar watching Mick Jagger on
video and feel sort of sad and mushy and a little bit
guilty, do we?
And people might call us sadistic for wondering how long
she can really stand up
There she goes again her arms flailing around — what do
arms mean? Reaching? I want? Give me . . . I'm dying,
give me
And the applause the audience's applause how
melodramatic the applause that killed her
Too melodramatic I'm staggering into my drink it's late
I'm thinking of you and an alley and you probably knew
I'd get into an alley it's all a pretense writing a poem
about Judy Garland
It's really a poem about you and what I wonder is do you
remember? You probably remember
Do you think someone heard us? Does it matter? Were
we being silly? Are you actually an evil manipulator? Can
you actually believe I find you INTERESTING? And
dramatic? Has anyone ever written a poem for you
before? This poem has gone on too long
I should get back to Judy Garland
Here I am standing in a bar watching a little faggot dance
under a video of Judy Garland
He is very stoned
So am I
I'm thinking about you
and Judy Garland
Interesting combination

EIGHT POEMS OF ADVICE FROM A FRENCH WHORE TO A YOUNG, HANDSOME, FLIRTATIOUS COWBOY EMBARKING ON A CAREER IN LITERATURE

1. Merci beaucoup je suis tu es il est elle est nous sommes
vous êtes ils sont elles sont avez vous un plume de ma
tant amour buckets oui oui oui ou no ou maybe

2. Can't think of what to say really
'cause you've got a car and a coyote
and a dream
But someone like you shouldn't be let loose on the world
without a little advice
So here's some
Drive careful boy
but not too careful
and when you get stoned
write things
'cause it's on those lonely nights on the road
I mean range
when those cowboys really let loose
And then there's the bunkhouse
And what's really between your legs, huh?
Is it a dick?
Sorry I got out of control
But just you remember
when you sit on couches with venerable playwrights like
me
don't touch them cowboy
unless you want to get touched back

3. Be ambitious
but only for your work because
only work matters
Don't look at me like that with your big brown eyes
or are they blue
just don't
Ambition is this thing that will kill you if it's money fame
and power
But what doesn't kill you — everything does
But no listen don't laugh
you've got this thing this need
so do it want it
but want to create a world that's not real life because
what else is there to want
but what there isn't
And when they tell you that you have to learn about the
here and now and your fellow man and write about what
you know then get in your old mustang put the dog in
the front seat have a few tokes and drive off into the
prairies with your very own space aliens from Mars

4. Be promiscuous
but only with your body
The body
sorry bullshit your body
was made to be touched
especially your buttocks
(you wouldn't want to be touched there would you?)
Well sorry that's what bodies
are for

But your mind
your feelings
your emotions
they are for those special people who understand
they are for me
And if I seem aloof or distant or thoughtful or drunk
I probably am
But I'm probably wondering what it would be like if I
had everything if everything was mine and I can imagine
it late at night we've driven off somewhere it's a country
road flat the land is flat but not you have all these curves
and humps and hardnesses just proof that a cowboy is not
the prairies he's the opposite he goes up and down
And I'm caressing your incredibly thick legs
and the dog is in the backseat
with an erection
and the moon is full
The dog barks he wants you too
but he can't have you
We wrestle the dog and me over you
I'm dead ripped apart
he's chewing my bones
and later there will be vultures
but I will have had you
cowboy.

5. Don't say you didn't flirt
I don't care if you didn't flirt
Don't say you didn't flirt
because you flirted okay?
Saying you didn't flirt is the first
sign of flirting okay?

6. Do not hurt ladies
Don't lie to them
Don't turn up without calling
And by ladies I mean anyone who wears a dress
because you seem to go for that kind
the ones with makeup and hair
and nails and helplessness
ladies like me
But don't hurt us
We don't mind being devoured by dogs over you
but we don't like being left crying in cars
our dresses hiked up over our heads
We're pretty and we want to stay that way
And we're not cowgirls
we're different from you
we wear high heels and perfume and smell like Paris
Just because of some mother who didn't treat you right
and doesn't understand you
don't give everything in a dress a hard time
We like you hard
us ladies with our foreign accents
but only hard
down there

7. Mon petit . . . Milord . . . ne venez pas . . . restez ici . . .
s'il vous plait . . . je vous aime . . . je suis . . . empty . . .
sans vous . . . hallo . . . charmant . . . big one . . . Ne venez
pas! No no non!

8. And finally
Don't take advice
from elderly playwrights like me
who dream they are French whores
The ones who look at you at parties
and want to see you bare-assed
wearing nothing but your cowboy hat
Don't take advice from us
'cause we're whores after all
and there will be other cowboys
But this whore will always remember the one
who liked to drive away and never come back
and who laughed like my first best friend
and who touched me too much for a straight guy
and who wore pants that were too tight
and who had a very strange relationship with this dog
This whore is thinking about you now
and that means you are here
I close my eyes
there you are

The Speech I Should Have Made

All I remember is sitting at the table at my Dad's.
I must have been 14.
It was turkey or something.
The "men" were sitting around the table after dinner.
And his friend's name was Al.
(I guess all the "women" were knitting
or something)
So Al says, "What are you going to do with yourself, Sky,
when you grow up?"
And I said (bravely I realize, looking back on it now),
"I'm going to be a writer."
"A writer," says Al, pondering this.
"Yes," I say (I imagine my chin protruding proudly,
the way I've seen heroines in old movies do it).
Well, you'd think I'd told him I'd just got the part of the
fairy in the school play
(or something).
"Weren't all those writer guys, weren't they
homosexuals?" asks Al, screwing up his face.
Well gee whiz, I'm only 14 and I don't want to answer
that question. And Dad and Al are both watching me.
Like it was important or something.
"Well no, they weren't," I say. But I know I don't sound
very conclusive.
Pause.
"What about Shakespeare?" asks Al. "He was a homo,
wasn't he?"
"No," I say querulously, staring at my father. (HELP ME!
I'm thinking.)
He's a nice Dad. He tries.
"I've never heard Shakespeare was a homosexual," says Dad.

"Well I've heard he was," says Al. "All those writers, far as I know, were homosexuals."

These days, I'd say Al had what we would now call an "agenda."

I won't go on, because all I could do was deny, deny and I got very upset and when I went upstairs to masturbate in my father's house (which was always a guilty proposition) the whole affair was doubly worrisome. Nowadays I might have answered differently.

"Yes, homosexual," I would say. "And to paraphrase Baudelaire, be always homosexual, for it is blessed to be so, throw yourself into that ass, your face into that crotch, love always the young, for they are beautiful, and expect to be fucked and you will. Be queer, be gay, release your bodily fluids in plastic or over nakedness. Spend nights being homosexual, days being homosexual, spend languid hours, buried in the hair of a homosexual, love your own kind, be perverse. Look in the mirror, kiss it. Remain fixated at a certain spastic age; yes the age where love is still fresh and sex is still guilty and quick. Masturbate always, and when you do, think of yourself with those you shouldn't be with, naked. Yes, Al, to be a writer is to be a homosexual. Shakespeare, Edna St. Vincent Millay, even Henry Miller, were all homosexuals. In fact, Al, to be alive is to be a homosexual. You are a homosexual, Al, and so is my father. I'm going upstairs now, to masturbate. If I come down later for a snack, will you make sure and tell me who sucked off who, while the ladies were crocheting?"

And then I would run upstairs and then there would have been all that adolescent doorslamming.

Or something.

BAD PLAY

Why we're seven fags gathered at a country house
Hi, I'm Terasse McWilly
and I'm your playwright
This play is much better than that horrible and
homophobic BOYS IN THE BAND
We live in a nice house now
and none of us are pockmarked or Jewish!
Buttz hates himself, but not because he is a homosexual
only because he is fat and has AIDS!
We have much better reasons for hating ourselves now
I know what I'll do!
I'll introduce a character named . . . um lemme think
JOHN! — an angry and bitter British composer
and guess what
(new dramaturgical idea)
I'll never tell you why he's so unhappy!
(if I did, the movie might get complicated and we might
not sell tickets!)
So I'll just make all the other characters say he's awful
and then give him an outburst!
Oh yes!
I know
I'll get someone to say "nigger" at the table!
And let my incredibly stereotyped Latino sex bomb
character object to it!
No one could accuse me of *not* being controversial!
As for conflict
here's a new idea!
Someone will sleep with someone they shouldn't!
NEAT HUH!

And of course my modern 1990s homosexuals
unlike the BOYS IN THE B
have never heard of open relationships or parks or toilets
or bathhouses
so it will be instant conflict!!!
Oh I forgot to tell you
One of my characters is blind

Pity

Just to top it all off; I'll name my play BAD WRITING!
BORING MONOLOGUES! BATHOS! (with exclamation
points after everything!)
Wow!
You can bring the kids to see it!

WHY SITTING HERE WATCHING YOU DRINK COFFEE IN MY BED WEARING YOUR FAVOURITE WHITE BATHROBE OF MINE REMINDS ME OF MY GRANDFATHER

(for Shaun)

Well it does
Let me tell you a little bit about my grandfather
He wasn't really my grandfather, I mean
he was my grandmother's second husband and no relation
But he was always the kindest person I ever knew
I mean I knew Mom and Dad didn't really approve
They tried to understand why I rode around town with
my Raggedy Ann doll in my bicycle basket even though
the other boys made fun of me they tried to understand
And my dad tried to play baseball with me and talk
And my mother tried to get me to hold my wrists
straighter
But my grandfather who wasn't really my grandfather
he used to take me fishing
and taught me how to use a darkroom
and let me listen to his old classical music
But most of all he had this great old recording of "Sweet
Sue," you know "Sweet Sue, that's you!" on an old
scratchy record and usually once every visit he'd pull it
out and I'd put on my special little tap shoes and they'd
clear a space in the den and I'd do my little tap dance to
"Sweet Sue" and my grandmother used to clap and my
mother used to laugh and my father seemed, grudgingly,
to approve of this particular peculiarity of mine
And I knew, unbeknownst to them all (or maybe they
knew, hence the suspicions) who I imagined myself to be

I was Shirley Temple
and it was *The Littlest Colonel* or it was *Heidi* or it was
Little Miss Marker and whatever scrape I was in, I just
knew I could save the crippled boy and raise the money
for the orphanage if I just did a little tap dancing
You know I think deep down my grandfather, who wasn't
really my grandfather, knew that I wished I was thought I
was dreamed I was Shirley Temple and you know I think
he didn't really mind and I don't think he approved or
disapproved I think he just really loved me and liked it
And so I imagine that today, my grandfather, who wasn't
really my grandfather, was looking in on us, and he saw us
making lazy love in the morning light and he saw me make
you, a fine strapping young man, a really good cup of
coffee, because I like making my man a good cup of
coffee,
and then he saw you sitting on my bed reading porno
mags and watching old movies on TV drinking coffee and
wearing your favourite white bathrobe which was mine
And I think he even saw me loving you
And I think he didn't approve or disapprove or anything
he just loved me and really liked it
Do you think that's possible?

BEUYS

I had my choice
between Beuys
and boys
I don't know
Some choose Beuys
Peter did
As for me, though I find Beuys nice
I still choose boys
After all
when Beuys walks into the sea
you know it's because of Kierkegaard or Steiner
But boys
they're a different matter
They walk into the sea because the night calls them
because they're lonely
or because the sea is wet
And they don't . . . come back
I repeat, don't
So if I had my choice
I'd take boys
their thighs are bigger
and they don't come back
(sorry, Joseph)

Corners Lamay
(apologies to that great
gay poet: Thornton Wilder)

1. A Typical Day, in Lamay

Don't know what to say, really
Our town's pretty much like any other
I reckon most towns everywhere are the same
People are people, and that's the truth
The name of the town is Corners Lamay
Don't know why it's called that
Can't say
But people have always called it that
And everyone knows better
Than to ask why
As you can see
The lights are beginning to come up
In Corner's Lamay
Old Dr. Posh, he's getting out of bed
See him feel his back
That rheumatism is a-hurtin'
He's been pretty busy lately
There's young Denny Hilts
See, he's openin' up the door of
The Bit and Bite
They're running out of Irish Cream
That Irish Cream is very popular
It's always been that way
Ron Normand
Picks up his suitcase
Ready to leave for his day job

His cruising clothes are on the chair
He took 'em off in quite a hurry
Last night
The baths are pretty empty
They've cleaned out all the rooms
Except for the one where Ray Pitumi
Lies sleepin'
Last night he took some Ecstasy
Tricked once or twice
He'll probably sleep 'til noon
In the park
Josh Pardner
The slow kid they got to help out
He's cleanin' up the used condoms
And the beer bottles
It was a warm night last night
The park was busy
They told him to wear rubber gloves
He does what he's told
In their black bedroom
Snaz Bizarre
and her girl Giggly
are lyin' abed late
They've got a woman between 'em
A woman who calls herself Mummy
They found Mummy at Rumours, the night before
Mummy opens her eyes
And wonders where she got to
There's a bottle of almost empty poppers
Lying on the floor

2. Love in Corners Lamay

It's 12 o'clock noon
People have finally rolled out of bed
The Bit and Bite
Is pretty crowded
Ray Pitumi
Is workin' the room
He's not wearing a shirt at all really
His blue eyes gleamin'
Anybody want to sit with me?
Share my coffee?
Dr. Posh stops by
He's had a rough morning
Stirs his coffee
Looks around
At who's skinny, sickly
Who he might see next day in his office
Who's takin' care of themselves
Who's not
Snaz and Giggly
Bought Mummy a donut
They sure don't know how to get rid of her
Snaz has got a movin' job soon
Doesn't want to leave Mummy with Giggly
A bit too much chemistry there
It's a problem
Josh eyes Ray
Josh might be gay
If only he knew the meaning of the word

And then Norm rushes in
It's his lunch hour
He just has time to hurry down
And make eyes at young Denny
Doesn't think Denny cares for him
Denny doesn't know how to say it
But he wants a Daddy
"Would you like some extra cream?"
He asks Norm
And at that moment
At the Bit and Bite
At 12 o'clock
When there is no moon
When the sun is near its height
In the early autumn sky
With the babies from Hades
In the prams rushing by
Norm looks at Denny
And Denny looks at Norm
And Norm knows Denny wants a Daddy
And that Daddy might be he

3. Death in Corners Lamay

Three years have passed
And Denny and Norm have been lovers
For two
Denny doesn't work at the Bit and Bite anymore
Josh is working there

He had his first gay experience
He didn't understand it
But it was lots of fun
Giggly moved in with Mummy
Snaz got very violent
But after she threw some furniture 'round
She felt a lot better
Ray works at the bathhouse now
He tricks between shifts
He organized a drag show for Thursday nights
And Tuesday night pizza
People enjoy that
At the hospital
Dr. Posh closes
Norm's eyes
Norm just died from Kaposi's Sarcoma
Denny is at his side
Denny closes his own eyes
"Oh just let me live one day
Just one day over again
Let it be an ordinary day
The most ordinary day
No, let's make it the day
That I told Norm I loved him
Over the Irish Cream
Even tho' I didn't know it"
Yup
Love and death
And an ordinary day
Are the same as anywhere
In Corners Lamay

ON FAME

It was the Halloween Ernie said
"That year we lived in the same house
you were a great influence on me"
And the woman outside the theatre yelled
"You are a God!"
As I lurched towards Yonge Street in my high heels
Richard was being vicious
Or Eddie was being sensitive
It's hard for me to be sure
Bruno said "I've never seen you looking so beautiful"
Onstage I sang a song
Everyone clapped and seemed to think I was talented
It seems to matter little
As the thunder of the applause dies down
That James does not succeed in getting an erection
and pulls his limp dick out of my waiting ass
Holding the soggy condom he inquires
"Where should I put this?"
"Why, on the plush velvet cushion" I say
Being the queen that I am
It's not that I want to be loved by one particular person
or anything
That would be asking too much
It's kind of this trade you make
The respect of many
For the passion of one
And there might not have been a velvet cushion
when the sad and sorry fucking was done

IMITATION OF LIFE

It's the middle of the movie
The MOST melodramatic scene has just finished
It's the one where the young black girl goes to meet
Troy Donahue
(it must have been his first role, in 1959)
and it's one of those incredible Douglas Sirk alleys
(they don't exist in real life)
with a row of streetlights in the distance
and "BAR" written in big letters across the window behind
"Let's run away," the black girl says
"you wanted that job in Jersey"
Troy Donahue strings her along for a minute or so
but deep down he's just a bigoted white person
Suddenly he bursts out with, "Why didn't you tell me
your mother was A NIGGER!"
The music swells and it's that strident
jazzy rockish stuff that means beatnik
and what have we come to sleazy
in late fifties movies
and he starts hitting her
and all the time she's screaming
"I'm as white as you!"
But she ends up on her knees
crying in a pool of blood and garbage
and Troy Donahue runs off into the night
CUT
And suddenly we're in Lana Turner's
sumptuous livingroom
and Annie her black maid is massaging her feet

"That feels better, Annie," she says
and starts to put on her wildly impractical
high heeled bedroom slippers
(no wonder her feet hurt)
and what's so amazing is that
Lana is literally in another movie
They forgot to tell her *Imitation of Life*
was an important movie about racial prejudice
for all Lana knows this is still
The Postman Always Rings Twice
and the audience is waiting for her next outfit
well she's doing okay now
in the dressing gown with the fur collar
and now Lana's looking misty and talking about her past
and now Annie is telling Lana about her life
and Lana is lighting a cigarette
She doesn't care at all
about Annie's life as a black person
and neither do we, unfortunately
not while Lana's lighting that cigarette
Annie mentions her friends
"Oh," says Lana, "do you have friends?"
"Why yes," says Annie, who is very black
and usually sick (she dies later)
"I have friends at the Baptist church and at the lodge"
"Oh," says Lana, with a distracted look in her eyes
for she's a big movie star
playing a big movie star
and after all she has to juggle the fact that Fellucci
a big film director
(with a name that's a combination of Fellini and Gucci)

wants her to fly to Italy
and John Gavin wants to marry her
and through it all there's still the problems
of being very beautiful and very rich
"Oh," says Lana waving her cigarette
and looking off, thinking about her next big film deal
and her next knockout outfit
"I had no idea you had any friends"
"Well," says Annie, as reproachful as Annie can be
she is, after all, a black saint
"you never asked me"
And just as Lana's face is clouded over
for a second
in a flicker of guilt . . .

London Poem #1

Oscar Wilde said
Whistler created the fogs of London
I have snorted too many poppers
and can only write short lines
of poetry now
a young man at Oxford Circus
asked me about my muscles
I miss you
and I'm tired of travelling
you are every boy I ever wanted
you are every man I ever met
until I actually return
and see you again
then we'll see what kind of boy
you really are

LONDON POEM #2

Constable painted lots of clouds
over 100 of them
all he had to do was look up
fences and stones
crushed glass atop a wall
a Mercedes in an alley
my pierced tit hurts
and my anus is bruised
the South African who
shoved his hand up it said
"You're a bit messy, mate,
if you don't mind me saying,
nothing serious tho"
thank heaven
for manners

LONDON POEM #3

I was sick in a bar in Clapham
a fat girl wouldn't Karaoke
she had big sad eyes
I identified with her
aren't we just all
fat girls in Clapham
who will not Karaoke?
the skinny fag in the bad vest
tried to drag her up onstage
but Barbra Streisand she would not be
it's a bar for cripples
and stutterers
called The Two Brewers
I felt very comfortable there
home at last

LONDON POEM #5

beautiful labourer
pretty sailor
relax with me
you've worked very hard
your lashes are too long
and your sweat tastes good
rest with me
my young workman, come
lay in my arms
there is someone who understands
that speech is not important
only muscles
which move suddenly
and then are inexplicably quiet
let me hold you
kiss your sweating brow
my pretty sailor
oh, my beautiful labourer

London Poem #5 (Cardiff)

It's an English bathhouse
which means the taps don't run
or the water is scalding
you lie behind a half open door
I open it
and you take my cock in your mouth
it all happens quickly
but not quick enough
the fur on your stomach is beautiful
a roughness about your face
I will never see you again
it doesn't matter
was it a bad night for you
or a memorable one?
across the street some footballers shout
I am glad
that they are out there
and I am asking these questions
in here

London Poem #6

Hammersmith Bridge is very pretty
and yet the Irish tried to blow it up

leather bars are supposed to be kinky
but everyone is wearing the same thing

some of the most romantic moments I ever had
were in a toilet

if it hasn't happened already — someone in London
will kill someone else — in a fight about transit

Brighton is heroic
if only for pretending to have good weather

at first the guy seems like a nasty Irish dom
   with a big dick
but sex is over and he camps it up with a tea towel

if you complain about the TV in your B and B
they'll put you in a room with no view

the best restaurants
don't look very pretty on the outside

if a man tells you he has a big dick
it often doesn't seem to live up to expectations

decadence seems connected with fascism
but in fact they are opposites

an empty carousel with the wind blowing its cover
  on a cloudy day
is often more gorgeous than the same carousel
  going round on a sunny day

LONDON POEMS: EPILOGUE

I've got his lighter
it's on the desk
on the book
he left it
and I kept it
it doesn't smell like him or anything
but the memory of him is there
someday, it'll stop working
but it was his lighter
he held it
sometimes he'd yank it out of his pocket
and laugh
when I feel it
I can feel his hands on me
hands that knew what they wanted
strong hands that gave me pleasure
see now, it lies full in my palm
I flick it on

SOME DENIALS
(APOLOGIES TO DOROTHY PARKER)

I.

Speaking of your beauty
I've quite had my fill
I mean there won't be any need anymore for me to bring a
case of beer and drink it all while getting to know your
friends — all a pretence for kissing you
One can certainly have one's fill of beauty like yours
For, certainly, to imagine endless draughts of plump
buttocks and your youthful flesh hot beneath my hands
becomes boring after a while
Ah yes, even as I write this poem, I'm yawning
All I can say is, thank god it's over
Yawn

2.

In another city
I hear a particularly cloying song on the radio
Sentimental and romantic,
luscious with a sweep of dropping thirds
this music is obviously calculated to make me cry
Of course it's not you I'm crying about
Of course it's my lost youth, and being in a foreign
land, and my shoes are too tight and I had to try
particularly hard, harder than usual, to get laid last night
and I miss my cat

These are, quite obviously pressing concerns
which, conspiring with that sudden burst
of 11 a.m. San Francisco sun,
have engineered a predictable response:
the fantasy that I miss you
Knowing this is all the result of a collusion of precipitate
coincidental effects I am ultimately unmoved
Yes certainly I am crying, and I conjure up your desperate
yet detached 22-year-old kisses warm on my thigh
But these manufactured images soon disappear and I am
watching myself cry
And it is all rather comic, really

3.

Having had a lot of men and still thinking of you is the
stuff from which a certain kind of melodramatic garbage
is made
Certainly either tragedy or farce — I shall decide later,
which
Ah yes, familiar territory, it's as if the image of you,
passionate, bored, the image of you perhaps picking your
feet, is so potent, that it travels unalloyed across time and
distance — pungent, sweat filled, perorated with longing,
wet
with a certain remembered allegory of some image of
youth, of eagerness, of confusion, of conceit which is your
personality which I imagine I desire as much as your body

Honestly
You'd think I'd read it all somewhere or made it up

As if the remembered image of yourself, MR. BEST, in
some sort of preoccupied repose, could actually bridle my
never-ending, ever-changing, obsessive promiscuous
desires for
other boys
Or worse yet, satisfy me?
Even the remembrance of you,
sweet enough to satisfy me
Hah
It is, after all, a ridiculous concept

4.

Incongruous with lust and remembrance I, a caped
crusader of semi-virile ilk, sip cappuccino in a room
resplendent with diced queens on coke,
bitter they are, and redundant (or did I say that already?)
déjà vu on the big screen spread eagled bare-breasted
(yes you kissed them repeatedly, dare I mistake
it for more than duty?) and nonsense seems
riddled with the enigma of Russia, wrapped in it, like the
revelation that Winnie the Pooh was a bear found in
Ontario, brought to England, and that A.A. Milne was
not a pederast
Inarticulate with envy for your next lover, I am,
yours truly, denying all, love, me

5.

I don't want you
I don't need you
I don't regret the flip and perhaps inappropriate postcard
I sent you
When I return home I will have no need to call you
I certainly have no desire to see you perform in a play
and am not at all interested in whether or not you are
a talented actor
I have absolutely no intention to lick your bum or to
enjoy you licking mine

Whether or not you comb your hair or wear short shorts
that barely cover your ass
is completely a matter of indifference to me
I can't even remember the colour of your eyes
Your hair was brown, wasn't it?
It seems to me you laughed a lot
Funny, I just can't seem to remember

6.

So this afternoon I will go to a leather-bar tea dance, and
there will be lots of hefty and beefy older men there, men
with experience, tact, men who are good in bed and know
who they are and what they want, which is, more often
than not, me.

And I will have a chance to meet someone my own age,
settled, with similar interests and experience, someone
who will see me as a love object instead of the other way
around. What relief. To socialize with men of a certain
age and substance. I'm glad I've grown out of this
obsessive-boy-thing. After all it was only a phase,
probably somehow related to a deep inner self-loathing.
But I'm over it now, thank you.

7.

Not your lips
Not your ass
Certainly not the way you talk or laugh or sit carelessly
in a chair
Not your dizzy tendency to forget to call
Not your lack of any real interest in me
No
        None of these things

8.

And I am the Queen of Rumania

How Beauty Is Like Eating
a Chicken Salad Sandwich

Wake me, I am sleeping
Wake me
Tho' it seems I go about my daily tasks with stunning
regularity
Tho' I seem to know why I exist and exactly where I'm
going
Tho' it seems I work and scrimp and save and blow it all
on some holiday
I'm sleeping
Wake me
I am reminded of an incident at the London Apprentice
backroom where I was displaying my tits and my erection
and a lad with a shaved head approached, produced a huge
cock from his striped shorts — which I sucked on —
and then he played with me until I came
"Well," he said, zipping up, hauling it all back in,
"at least you woke me up. I was falling asleep"
And that's what it's like isn't it?
You're fast asleep and dreaming
And all you want is to be woken up
to feel touch taste and hear again
Knowledge is sleep
Analysis is sleep
But oh to be awake again to find that in the moment
stretched like cellophane over lunch you punch through
and there is chicken salad which isn't a preparation for
anything else it's not an appetizer it's just dinner and it
just is and it's delicious

45

So
Tho' I may walk about with wary eye and care
Tho' I may slowly choose my step
and speak only when I dare
Tho' I may wait and worry, plan and concentrate
What I want most is
to be awake
Again
Wake me, beauty
For I am asleep

AND THE ROCKS SPEAK

It was night, in Cardiff
Trevor said they were the oldest rocks in the world
he said that the rocks speak
and then, later, he sat in the courtyard
looking quite like a fairy; a white light burning
a halo into his
fuzzy white hair
I got drunk of course
and nocturnal recreation called
Paul was a costume designer
and it wasn't long before he had
dragged me out to Bute Park
and we were rolling around in the twigs
under the Welsh moonlight
there's something about having your ass against a tree
and sucking on the full uncut cock
of a drunken Welsh boy
that puts things into perspective
a staggering leprechaun approached at one point
I could barely make him out through the fragrant,
luminous mist
he proved to be a soused old faggot
who finally fell asleep near us in the brush
and commenced to cough quite resoundingly
and annoyingly
as if on cue
Paul and I got very dirty
in a Welsh wood

And Trevor was right
the rocks were speaking to us
They said to me:
Sky, it's true you're forty-three years old, but you've
got a great cock, a hot body, and a terrific personality,
what you need is a big hairy boy who loves you
and is not afraid of getting a twig or two up his ass
I dragged Paul back to the guesthouse
and we snogged 'til morning, when I booted him out
The landlady at the guesthouse
found dirty sheets
and a floor covered with woody debris
she didn't clean
Was it a reproach?
I didn't listen
for when the oldest rocks in the world are explaining
who you are,
even the resolute click click of a landlady's tongue
falls quiet

CONFESSION NUMBER ONE

Alright, one more
And this is an early movie
One of the earliest *The Postman Rings Twice*
In *Postman* Lana is almost quadruply outclassed by the
terse, dark script, by the taut direction and by Cecil
Kellaway and John Garfield both consummate actors
with real talent
But Lana has something that outclasses everything and
everyone
The camera loves her in a way that reminds us of what
love is all about for just as our eye constantly turns to the
loved one to devour to observe every detail every batting
of an eye of flinch of muscle the camera cannot get
enough of her and she knows it when she says "I've never
been homely but ever since I was fourteen I've never met
a man who didn't give me an argument" and that beauty
always wins
Evil again, she pouts and plans but most of all she offers
her lips her eyes her hips and those outfits of classic
white (a different one in every scene) there is so much to
savour there's Lana bursting out of the diner in the dead
of night in her swimming garb, hair perfectly coiffed and
swinging her bathing cap with daring insouciance. What
is more daring even than sex with John Garfield under the
moonlight is going swimming with that hairdo
Will it get mussed?
But no, the blindness and faith of moviegoers in the '40s
was such that Lana could endure sickness death and even
midnight skinny dipping without damaging that hair
And in the silence of his bedroom

For at the crucial moment she slips into John Garfield's
bedroom and John Garfield registers for us the ecstasy
the surprise the utter delightful confusion of such beauty
suddenly appearing in one's bedroom
And Lana quivering there her shoulders hunched
intensely as we imagine the fall of her breasts the nipples
delicately grazing the starched white cotton fabric
"A woman needs love."
Yes Lana, yes like John Garfield we forgive your
ambition, we forgive your lies your plotting your
planning we even forgive your fake movie ironing
because we want to kiss you the way we want to kiss that
person we shouldn't, you know the one that every
instinct tells us will lead to sleepless nights and bad
phone calls and a general difficulty in dealing with
anything that's supposed to be important
We want to kiss you the way John Garfield does
And we know that he's whispering to himself
"I must . . . I must . . . even if it means my own . . .
someone else's death . . . I must kiss her . . . I must . . ."
He grabs her shoulders her muscles tense, the lips pout
and they plunge into the darkness, the oblivion, the
ecstasy which is their lust

LUSH, BUT NO MOON

1. Okay, let's get this cleared up right away. His name. Okay I'll just say it. I'm as ashamed of his name as I am of having lived in Buffalo at one time (another B-word). Okay it's Brent. Yes, Brent. Let's face it, if it's 1995 and you're sleeping with some guy in his early twenties he is going to be called the B-word. Brent or Bartley or Brandon. It's very difficult to get poetic and effusive about somebody named Brent. So let's just get this whole Brent thing out of the way now. Okay everyone say it with me, and if there's any laughter we'll have to say it again: Brent.

2. So I walk into this bar in Key West called Bourbon Street (the name is an excuse to have Mardi Gras parties at the slightest provocation). There's Brent sitting on a bar stool. And he keeps looking at me. And I keep looking at him. And so we pick each other up.

3. He's got short spiked hair. He looks like your average beautiful teenager: dark, with bright eyes. You look at him and think: he'll be hard. Everywhere. You just know it. Some boys you just look at them and know. They're hard. And his T-shirt said LUSH.

4. So he comes over and asks me for a light and of course I know this is a come on and I ask him about his T-shirt and it's here the generation gap begins. LUSH *is a band.* He looks at me, incredulous. Well of course I should know it's a band but I'm forty-three years old and the last three CDs I bought were musicals by Kander and Ebb and

Chita Rivera was in two of them, but of course I'm not going to tell him that. I'm going to try and bluff it, so I do. LUSH, hmmm I've never heard of them, what kind of music do they play anyway? This is a dangerous thing to say, but I really want this kid and he rhymes off three other bands I don't know and finally mentions the Red Hot Chili Peppers (you don't have to be hip to know them every old faggot knows them because they've been around for eons and they perform with socks on their cocks) and so I get all political about the Red Hot Chili Peppers because it's one of the only things I know how to be, political, and I say, Gee when is Flea going to come out of the closet anyway, and Brent says, *Oh he has, he's said he's bisexual.* Well I'm not going to argue the point, for me saying you're bisexual doesn't actually constitute coming out, but that just shows how old-fashioned I am and I'd better not say it 'cause it's contentious, so I don't. Thank the LORD I've actually heard of one of the bands he knows. So now we can get off the bands and it doesn't matter anyway 'cause as far as I'm concerned LUSH isn't the name of a fucking band it's his name. I never liked Brent anyway, and lookit him, just lookit, he's so LUSH.

5. So we talk about this and that. Who knows what I came up with to entertain him, and he says, Let's go sit with my friend and I think oh here comes the dumpster, this is the dumpster line, I'm going to end up in the scrap heap with all the arthritic, whining, *there's too much ice in my drink and I'd like a table near the window please, honey,* ancient homosexuals. But no, he actually wants to get rid of his friend and he goes with him off to the 801 and I sit and wait.

6. Oh God it's endless. I am this close, this close to having LUSH; but of course he could get away still, he could disappear into the piano stylings of the 801's never-ending cocktail hour and never return. And so I think I'll just finish this drink and if he doesn't turn up, I'll go to the video store and wank off with some sexy stranger from Kalamazoo. But I'm pretty certain he'll come back. And I'll tell you why.

7. It's this weird thing. He was listening to everything I said and I was talking a lot, but he wasn't really interested. And as I watched him not listening to me, I thought about all the times I'd sat with people and not really listened to them, but pretended I was. And the reason I did it was because I simply desperately wanted to fuck them and it didn't matter what they said. And I couldn't believe this kid this beautiful American boy in a LUSH T-shirt was so fucking horny for me that he could NOT listen to me for so long, with such intensity.

8. Yeah, he comes back. And then I touch his knee and say, Hey, if you sit this close to me any longer I've just got to kiss you, and I do. This does not seem to bother him. I'm going crazy so next I try, So do you want to go back to your place or my place. He had told me he lives around the corner and he knows I'm staying in a gay guesthouse called The Lighthouse Court which is kinda like a bathhouse. So he says, Do you want to go skinny-dipping, and I say, Well sure. Are you crazy? I think. Of course I want to go skinny-dipping with you, let's relive an adolescent memory I never even got to have, while we're at it why don't we circle jerk and read *Playboy*. So then I say, You mean skinny-dip at

Lighthouse Court? And he says, No, that would turn into a group scene. And he's right it would, I'm so glad to hear he doesn't want that, and then he says, Let's go down to Atlantic Shores. And I say is it closed now? He says, Yes, and then he says, We can just jump the fence.

9. So we walk down. But let me tell you a little bit about Atlantic Shores. It's this motel right on the water with a pool in it and a pier that goes way out into the ocean and it's like under the stars — it is. And so I know he's talking about sex under the stars on the pier in Key West. Fuck.

10. I can't remember what we talked about on the way down. I remember I talked a lot and he was intently not listening. It made me very horny.

11. So then we jump the fence and walk, no run, to the end of the pier and he's already taking his clothes off and fuck he's got a big hardon. Shit, my hardon is never big and I don't even know if I can get one. This intimidates me terribly and then I think, try not to see his instant hardon as intimidating, try and see it as a compliment. And we're about to step into the ocean naked and I'm thinking this is crazy and I laughingly say — Are there sharks? But I kind of really mean it and Brent I mean LUSH laughs and says, We'll find out. And then I think fuck we don't really want to go skinny-dipping we want to fuck which was my first really rational thought of the evening and I drag him onto the pier again and start sucking his cock. And things go crazy and I sort of won't tell you the details except that he seemed to love holding me, this big guy, and kissing me, and it was fabulous and he didn't come but I did but that was okay because I

could tell he could have come about five times and I
actually started having fantasies that he didn't want to
come with me because it might be just too big a thing for
him, which shows you how crazy I was.

12. So what does this all mean anyway? It means that like
every other gay tourist I went down to Key West feeling
like a lonely undesirable lump and came back fulfilled
and sexy as hell. Which makes it an ideal resort. Of
course we won't discuss why I had to go all the way
down there to find LUSH and discuss Flea and go out on a
pier 90 miles from Cuba to experience all this.

13. And it means one final thing. That I'm still romantic
about promiscuity. And that is a very important part of
me. I mean to a lot of people promiscuity is simply
having a lot of sex — that's why I don't understand
couples. There are a lot of couples looking for sex in Key
West, which is fine. But it's not my thing because how can
you have a romantic fantasy about a couple you're having
sex with, I mean you're obviously never going to fall in
love with a fucking couple and buy a house together. It's
just sex. Well, it may be too many Kander and Ebb
musicals, but I need the romance of promiscuity. And oh,
I forgot to tell you, at one point we looked up at the sky,
which was filled with stars, and it looked like you could
see the whole universe except there was no moon, which
was weird because we knew there had been a crescent
moon the night before and LUSH and I thought hmm, no
moon. And I thought that was significant. Yes, I spent my
night on the pier under the constellations with LUSH —
but there was no moon.

14. And I had one final question. Is that the way it's always going to be for me: LUSH, but no moon? And sometimes I think that's a stupid sad question and I shouldn't think it, and then other times I think you're forty-three years old and you've gone through a lot of shit and thank God I still ask questions like that. Thank God I still ask. You know?

A Poem for You and Frank O'Hara

I can't think of anything to say really
except that you left me the wrong socks
which is charming of you
Also Wednesday night will you be beautiful and eloquent
as expected? And impress all my friends?
I almost lost your phone number
If there's anything I don't like it's
not having you here in front of me right now
O singing alligators!
O running water!
I've never eaten pie as delicious as your smile and never
put my hands in gooey fingerpaint as nice as your curly
hair since General Franco gave up Spain
But I don't want to give you up ever
or until the end of February
Then again, March
you little soldier

ANGELS

1. Very popular right now.

According to *Time* magazine
we are seeing a resurgence of angels.
Who can account for the unprecedented popularity
of these winged cherubs?
Could it be a return to spiritual values?
Red-faced,
Ruddy,
Like real children
Except that their penises and clits have been brutally
Chopped off
By painters and sculptors offended by such plush,
redundant,
resplendent appendages.
Angels —
soft, cuddly, sweet, divine, laughing, gurgling, cooing,
waxing waning, never
complaining, pink, dimpled, chubby, draped in white
never see the dark of night,
peering over a cloud at break of day, the gates of heaven,
ah for the imagined innocence of a prepubescent smile
ah, for a smile worth violating

2. I like angels

Also.
I like to see them going at it.
You know.
I like to see angels fucking.
They don't look so goddamn cherubic then.
Dirty grimy bloodstained angels,
smelling of shit and semen
(does semen smell?)
they sniff each other's assholes
assholes redolent and hairy
oops a cling-on!
angels in dirty underwear
an angel with a hardon
when pink turns purple
dimpled cheeks strain
with desire
"Jesus Christ!"
they cry,
these little dappled whores
fucking on a cloud is kinda
like a waterbed
and all that water
kinda makes a girl wanna piss
open your mouth honey
this angel is gonna drop a load on you.
What kind of load?
Don't know
Let me open up. See what comes out.
Ughghg.

3. There I am, having a hot chocolate,

at the Second Cup
not even feeling attractive.
He sits down.
Hi.
Very blonde from Belleville just broke up with his lover
who he still lives with
but he's not rushing into anything, says he.
Meanwhile, I have barely had time to say hello.
No, let's not rush into anything, angel, I think.
"I can't,
because of my condition," he says.
What condition?
I ask.
"I'm HIV positive," he says.
Ah.
Doe eyes
brown eyes, my little HIV positive angel
I look down
ahh, yes
strangely enough
you do have a penis
let me touch it
ahh
Let's see what comes out.

Madame X

The depth of Lana's suffering knows no bounds
in *Madame X*
a sublime achievement
for in so many movies Lana played a bad girl
or an innocent woman
But here it's the perfect combination
Yes, evil enough
(laughing and being witty with Fernando Lamas
while her husband is busy
again, the husband has no time for her)
But then she is tricked into murder by her evil
mother-in-law (Constance Bennett plays Lana's
mother-in-law but looks younger than her)
And because of this foul she-trick must flee
as she says to Christian, the Swedish conductor who
loves her unselfishly, beautifully
and with an accent
"Love is for the living, I am already dead"
And as if to prove it she piles on heaps of pale base and
eyebrows and lines to age her
The amazing fact being of course that Lana is
in actuality
the same age as the dissipated woman she ends up playing
Though to play her without makeup would be
unthinkable
We never ever get to see Lana's real face
even though her own lines might be appropriate
Lana is bad but not really bad
good but not really good

and we see ourselves in her suffering
For have we not all been wronged?
Has not nature or chance or circumstance
dealt us a bad hand
And haven't we paid for it bitterly?
(Lana lying face down in a hotel room bed
— her drunken sleep —
the man she picked up last night
a stranger rifling her purse for money)
And yet when we are gnashing our teeth
and pounding the bed
isn't there just the slightest tinge of guilt?
(I deserve it)
Think of the unabashed sentimentality of it all
for at the heart of everything Lana is a mother
(aren't we all?)
and at Christmas time
even though she is addicted to absinthe
and heavy eyebrow pencil
and Burgess Meredith is trying to make money off her
and she's been wearing the same tacky flowered robe for
three days (well, it *is* Mexico)
Lana looks off into wherever actresses look
when they are dreaming of better days
and says "My son . . . he was more than just a son . . . he
was a prince . . ." and her eyes cloud and we know she
means it
Lana's secret?
She believed in all that sentimentality
more than the meager wit in her scripts
more than the improbable stories
and more than the outrageous costumes

More than her press releases
she believed that the most important
relationship in the world
is the one between a mother and her child
and for a moment, watching her in her Mexican hovel
when we're not trying to figure out
what is the light source
for the weird green spot that is showering her
platinum blonde hair
yes, we too believe

WHY KATHIE LEE GIFFORD IS JUST
LIKE THE UNITED STATES OF AMERICA

She's mean
She's greedy
She's very very pretty
And of course she's a lying hypocrite
And of course she's on TV every morning
And just like America, Kathie Lee Gifford is a drag queen
And what's a drag queen?
Well, someone who just can't stop drawing attention to
how pretty they are — I mean Kathie Lee, every time she
moves her legs or bats an eye or touches her hair, she
reminds you, in that subtle way she has, of how beautiful
she is and yes okay so she *is* beautiful but more than that
each gesture says I'm beautiful, so beautiful. And that I'm
barely, just barely, conscious of it. And on top of that I'm
intelligent (questionable) and vicious. I can be vicious. If
I have to, I can defend myself against anything and I'll
still be beautiful: oooh I'm just stamping my little high
heels right now and removing a stray lock of hair with
my long long dangerous fingernails. Yes I can stand up
for what I believe and be glamorous too
And I believe in America (which means myself)
Kathie Lee Gifford
And I believe in fidelity and marriage and love (and all
the other lies)
And even when you find my husband's fat hairy wrinkly
old dick up some forty-five-year-old Exercise Queen in a
hotel I can pull my life back together and lie
Like drag queens and the United States of America
I can lie

I can exploit Latina women in sweat shops and then I can
appear with President Clinton and I can lie
And you will love me, Kathie Lee Gifford
You will
But most of all, you will watch me on TV
Because that's the way mornings are
Inescapable, the beginning of all that treachery and
drudgery and then there's me, being more beautiful than
you'll ever be
Look at me
I'm Kathie Lee
I'm some kind of an achievement

SOME INCIDENTS THAT HAPPENED
ON MY SUMMER VACATION

1. IN NEW YORK CITY at the Universal Restaurant with all
the upscale fags drinking and being trendy and it was
someone's birthday and they put on an old disco song
and pulled out a cake and a cute waiter put on a hat and
lip-synched and there on a cold night in February amidst
all the AIDS deaths and suffering and my friend a young
writer who wanted my opinion on his play so I took
advantage of him and his social set for one night turned
and said to me, "It doesn't get gayer than this, does it?"
True.
But actually it does really because later I went to this
sleazy little fuck club called PRISM on 9th Avenue you
just get out of the cab, you don't look around and found
myself after eight beers with my ass in the air and a huge
black stud slapping it shoving ether under my nose
yelling, "TAKE THAT ON YOUR BIG WHITE BUBBLE BUTT!"
while several fags watched.
Oh Mark, I beg to differ but it did get gayer than that.
It did.
So after being suitably chastised for being in possession
of a big white bubble butt, it was time to go visit my
father.

2. IN CONNECTICUT things were quieter. I love my dad
but he watches TV a lot. And he tried so hard he'd been
reading up about theatre and he asked me questions. But
basically we watched a lot of TV. And even though there's
four TVs, one in the living room one in the bedroom, one
in the den and one in the DINING ROOM, believe it or not,
the DINING ROOM, still, we had TV wars. I just could not

watch tennis or golf. So there was me in the living room
watching TO HAVE AND HAVE NOT it's not really a very
good movie except for "PUT YOUR LIPS TOGETHER AND
BLOW" did Hemingway write that line? I doubt it.
Anyway, Dad, Stepmother, and Stepgrandmother are
huddled in the den watching tennis. Oh I felt so guilty!
And horny. So at one o'clock in the morning when all
were long asleep I locked myself in the downstairs john
and jerked off on the toilet. Which was okay, cleaned up
frantically and flushed, then the next day I took a shit in
the same toilet and of course it wouldn't flush. Oh no.
Stopped up and four or five big light brown turds
floating around in it, impervious to my anxiety. An
impervious turd, what an oxymoron. Anyway, I
nonchalantly strolled to the living room to watch TV and
sneaked back ten minutes later to try again but no luck
no flush, ambled innocently back to watch TV —
suddenly my stepmother emerges from the john, "The
toilet's plugged up!" Well you've never seen such
excitement, she and my father run to the toilet to examine
my turds. "I did it," I confess. I wouldn't want them to
think that those horrible shits belonged to Granny, she
gets in enough trouble for being senile and fucking up her
knitting, poor old gal. "Sky," says my stepmother, who is
a registered nurse, "why didn't you tell us?" Well, this is
my big moment, I think, I can be honest. Bare my soul. "I
didn't tell you," I say, "because I was embarrassed."
"Oh," says my stepmother, sizing me up in that
condescending fraught with deep not so hidden hatred
Nurse Ratched sort of way that drives me insane, "why
would you be embarrassed?" because of course she is a
nurse and is just so goddamned comfortable with bodily
functions. Hah! I think Hah! If you knew I'd jerked off

on the same toilet last night you'd have a fucking heart attack. You love looking at my shit, but one look at my cum and you'd be screaming bloody murder, like somebody knifed you. Anyway, Dad unplugged the toilet, things calmed down and it was time to watch the six o'clock news.

3. IN KEY WEST Last night I went to Aunt Lolly's Corner Grocery Store to buy some beer. And Aunt Lolly asked me for ID. I couldn't believe it! I was so happy! "I'm thirty-nine years old, Aunt Lolly!" I beamed. "Well," she said, "tell me your birthdate." I did. She handed me the beer. "Can't be too careful," observed Aunt Lolly. "We get a lot of spring-breakers in here!" Oh! Aunt Lolly — you made an old fag so happy!

4. IN KEY WEST So he was young blonde and sadistic as my postcard said and he made me think why oh why are people LIKE that. Certainly a little healthy sadism at the right time is okay but I picked him up at the Number One Saloon, he a southern boy cute accent, 29 yes, but eternally boyish Greg, sex is always good with a slender boy, even when it's bad, only problem he wanted desperately to fuck me without a condom. BUZZ warning signal, I should realize for future reference that in 1992 this is psychotic behaviour. Anyway needless to say I didn't let him, but fisted him instead. We talked he seemed actually charming but I am easily charmed by those of his ilk. Gave him my address in Key West, he said he'd drop by next day. Next day I woke early thinking of him, gussied myself up, didn't floss, waited, then noticed that he had left my address on the table. Oh

well. Went to the beach, who should be there but him. We chat. Rub oil on each other, make the other fags on the beach talk. Next, lunch he pays he proves to be a spoiled rich kid originally from Atlanta, he abuses the waitress in a charming way he obviously hates women and he's reminding me of my exboyfriend, pretty enough to get away with murder. I invite him back to my place Jeffrey Dahmer is on Geraldo oddly enough we start making love while watching Geraldo's tasteless tabloid interview with Dahmer's last almost victim we make jokes about it all, move to the bedroom. Sex is enjoyable but he keeps pushing his fingers up my butt, not in a nice way, not even in a nice fisting way, I mean it starts out nice and as soon as it feels good he starts hurting me, and I realize as he gazes into my eyes that he's enjoying this, enjoying my very real discomfort. I am not. Sex over he gets dressed will I see you tonight and he's gazing at me in that way someone does when they're falling for you. Gosh this is flattering but frightening, I say we can start boozing together at 10:30 at the 801 he agrees. Oh God the way he looks at me scares me half to death — you can't adore me yet you don't know me — we meet later he seems a tiny bit drunk not much, is gazing at me too much after two vodkas he suddenly is staggering falling asleep at least semi-permanently on the barstool, he says "You're a really hot man, you know?" again I'm very flattered but so sad he had to get this polluted just to say it. Then he punches me. Not hard but as he drifts into oblivion he gazes at me dreamily and punches my chest my thigh I realize that it is his attraction to me this big guy that he can't handle, desires me greatly but definitely wants to hurt me how sad how sad I leave him asleep on the barstool I hope he's okay.

5. IN KEY WEST I realize I am aurtistic, that's a combination of artistic and autistic. What do I mean by this — well autism is described by ex-autistics as being a state where everything hurts, every human contact, a caress becomes a blow a punch, the scrape of sandpaper on skin love equals dermabrasion and with me it's when people love me when I try to love them I am so overwhelmed by all their needs tortured trying to fulfill them please them I get afraid run from the intimacy so I can only relate to those who need nothing want nothing no guilt no pressure ultimately no relationship I must work on this problem or perhaps I can't oh well at least I wrote all this down that's the artistic part.

6. IN KEY WEST I write a poem:

THE NIGHT I DREAMED RICKY RICARDO WAS MY FATHER

Well it's possible.
I mean time-wise and all.
Well when Lucy was pregnant and in the hospital on TV
so was my mother.
I was born about one month before Little Ricky.
And I was early.
And I'm very dark and musically talented but a bit wacky
and I had a drum
set which I never played when I was a kid.
So like it's possible really maybe he was and in my dream
I'm sitting looking
at him at Ricky Ricardo senior and he's sitting in one of
those grand southern
cane backed chairs and he's wearing a tux but the tie is

casually off to the
side and he's so fucking attractive and we're chatting and
I can't believe it
he is my father!
And suddenly my whole life has changed because my dad
isn't this lovable
balding fat sexless old man.
He's young and horny with bright dark eyes
And of course I understand how I got like this how I got
this permanently
hard dick this libido from hell it's from Dad from Ricky
and it all makes sense.
It's nice to have a reason for being the way you are
And having a dad that understands you know?

Now I just have to deal with the fact that Lucy is my
mother.

On the Bus to New York City
(for Grant and Ruthann)

I hope they're dykes, not sisters
on the bus to New York City.
The fat one there is Gertrude Stein;
the thin one Alice B.
I hope they bump pussies into the night pressing large
hands into
strange forests of damp thighs and roll, and one runs
from the other crying, it's a summer afternoon — it's a
lesbian melodrama — "You love her more than me!"
As if anyone could ever be secure ever, but none ever
seem quite as content and set in their ways as those two
grey-haired ladies sharing cookies on the bus. Sometimes
I dream of becoming a lesbian, sometimes just to get close
to Grant, my new friend who, though born white, was
found by lesbians, in the woods, raised by lesbians, and
now he is of lesbian ways. Lesbians who sit up all night
talking about the sex they are going to have tomorrow
night but when they do have it, when those big hands go
exploring ooooooh ahhh thighs open clench and there's
no more talking.
If we could be lesbians would that mean we could share
cookies on a bus someday?
I hope for our sake
that they're not sisters.
I hope they're lesbians
on the bus to New York City.
And the thin one can be you
and the fat one can be me.

MASS IN B FLAT

prologue:

We call on Harvath, Grog, Enwhistle, Hundertwasser, the
great gods of the Vikes to bless this bastion this traveller
this floating emissary to the world beyond Gundrag,
Hipbath, Hondle, Hooper, Logo, Arat, Gods of heaven
sea and ships to guide this deadly mass upon its way.

introit:

what is it	what?
what is in this	in this?
in this bundle	this bundle?
this bundle of	bundle of
papers	paper
that we are burning	are burning
they belong to	belong to
a young lad	a mere lad
I said young lad	young lad
of twenty	twenty
how young	young

gradual:

Bless the lord for he maketh young men twenty years old
RESPONSE — For his mercy endureth forever
For he maketh them young, he maketh them randy, he
maketh them homosexual
RESPONSE — For his mercy endureth forever
For he maketh them lie in my bed and make strange
noises and giggle and hide their faces in the pillow and

read poetry and kiss and deny kiss and deny
RESPONSE — For his mercy endureth forever
Bless the lord for giving them brains as well as loins those
twenty-year-olds, but most of all for allowing them to
stay twenty for one whole year
RESPONSE — For his mercy endureth forever
Bless the lord for giving them the intelligence to laugh at
my jokes, the irony to see that I'm not always funny, the
vulnerability to apologize for being late, the lack of
experience to allow me to appear wise
RESPONSE — For his mercy endureth forever
But most of all thank the lord for girding their loins,
furring their thighs and strengthening their buttocks even
though no sign of earthly battle is imminent
RESPONSE — For his mercy endureth forever

tract:

A young man is nice
when he likes you
He's better it's true
when he loves you
But these things
(it must be said)
are usually decided in bed!
And bed
is a strange place
to think

dies irae:

Dies irae die ila solvet saeclum in favilla TESTES DAVID
CUM (shyly) sibilla

74

sanctus

What we have here is a pile of a glorious pile of papers
What is — what is in them? you may ask
The writings of a young man of barely twenty!
Ah!
What beauty what inarticulate inchoate testicular variety?
What divine anarchism, plunging masochism, plentiful
engorged playthings of the mind?
He wants to destroy these things because he has grown
out of them
Ah hah, we say, we know
Who knows?
For they were written before England, before Europe,
before Ceylon
Ah hah!
Alack and alas
When he was a teen?
Are we eager?
Do we preen to see what is about to be burned?
But no, like the pile of books in the woodshed, like the
teddy bear under the sofa, like the wad of Kleenex beside
the bed, what is being burned shall never be seen by men,
God, or (heaven forbid) his mother

agnus dei:

Buried deep
Buried deep
Buried deep within him
Buried deep
Buried deep are secrets we shall never know
Secrets we shall never know

Adolescent secrets
floating on Lake Ontario
sailing off to Buffalo?
Secrets!
Secrets we shall never know
Search him high and
search him low
Secrets buried deep
within him!
Secrets we shall never know
(pause)
Take off your shorts

benedicamus domino:

Let us bless the lord for he certainly knew what he did in
making you
You couldn't have been a mistake, though my eyes might
be a mistake and my thoughts about you
We never flew, 'tis true, like these papers which are
disappearing somewhere into Northern Ontario
But still I discern somewhere nay further than that away,
over the mountain hidden somewhere in the way you
smile
and say "Yes" there is a shall we say . . . profundity?
Dare we? True love, like death answers yes when you least
expect it
You have all the attractiveness of a gun half-cocked and
your oneness baffles me, makes me humble, effective,
weak in the knees
Let us bless the lord for if he made a mistake in you, he
made a good one and he followed it consistently to its
mistaken end, giving you long eyelashes and this poetry to

send out to sea
If a fish finds it he may smell your eyes in the ashes, feel
your laugh, breathe in the odour of your generosity
Being a teenager is gone now!
Grow up
Take hold
The comedy turns to tragedy which when viewed through
long eyelashes looks like a particularly juicy episode of
Dynasty
Farewell teen years
It's your party
You can cry, if you want to

epilogue

Heth, Grent, Bumble, Ackerwathe, lords of fish and lords
of sea, bless this vessel, which though weak might make
it to Toronto Island
Remember that you can't kiss an eighteen-year-old
in broad daylight unless he's a different sex than you,
and that
makes life tough
Grunt, Saxe, Indlebung, Grath, Og, Mog, Gorgor take
your money, take your youth, take these poems, and run

As Sure As If

Longing is a kind of company
there is a generosity in it
a presence inside the ache
a gift
(standing on the subway and not thinking of you, sure,
earlier there had been something, but then: some skinny
boy with fuzzy hair and a receding hairline — he had
some girl pressed against a pole — and suddenly it was
you, jumping up and down in my livingroom and saying
"If you break my heart, I'll break your face" and
demanding we dye our hair, and it was your fierce
bravery against whatever it is that was killing you, as
something so evidently was, that I loved, very clearly, "I
have a lesion on my nose" you said, I didn't bother to
ask, I was afraid to ask, why you used that word, *lesion*)
I have a feeling you'll turn up
But meanwhile,
there is, like a cold blast of wind in the face,
that whisper, when the cat makes a strange scurrying
sound,
the certainty of my longing,
which places you here beside me
as sure as if

PORTRAIT IN BLACK #2

In *Portrait in Black*, Lloyd Nolan is very clear about it
Lana has done nothing for the
first five minutes of the film
except pose in her oriental style dress
and look off into the distance
and her first shot is pure Lana
she is looking out the window, sadly, one expects
for though a lousy actress in every traditional respect
Lana is capable of acting with her back
gazing out the window when Richard Basehart says
"Sheila"
she turns
turns are Lana's best thing
surprised, shy, feminine, lonely
but so utterly utterly beautiful
Lloyd Nolan her husband is very clear about it
she has a love deficiency
a deficiency of love, that's her disease
It always was Lana's disease
if only she had been loved enough
then maybe things would have turned out differently
But no one ever in any movie anywhere
ever seems able to love Lana enough
She wants to take driving lessons
Lloyd Nolan her ailing husband finds out
"Where do you want to drive?" he says
grabbing her much more forcefully than a dying man
should be able to

"Why nowhere" she lies (searching, searching)
"to the hairdressers, stores, friends
I don't know I haven't given it much thought"
After all she is just a typical suburban woman
more rich and beautiful perhaps than most
But what she has to put up with
an ailing loveless husband
Wouldn't it drive you to murder?
And the child — Lana always has one in these movies
always so innocent as to appear retarded
oh there she goes again
nothing but music and a white room
and Lana, crying
Crying, her second best thing
She drags herself up
wipes away a tear
moves to the telephone
But first, a cigarette

THE MOMENT I MISSED YOUR LIPS

I had been waiting to meet you because
you were a composer and we had both been
rejected by the Canadian Opera Company
bespectacled, uptight, with a family, and doing part-time
work for the choir, that was the way I imagined you
and then
there you were
leaning up against something
at the corner of Ontario and Rue St. Denis
you were smoking weren't you?
all in white
and it seemed that you couldn't speak English very well
except that you could
and what do I remember most about dinner?
I remember there were a lot of pauses
pauses in which I fully expected you to get up and leave
but you didn't
you just sat there, looking beautiful
challenging me with those full fleshy lips
"I dare you I dare you to tell me how beautiful
my lips are"
and I took the dare
after a long long dinner
(my dinners never take three and a half hours)
in which you ate two hamburgers
and smoked two packs of cigarettes
(constantly cigarettes touch your lips
scrape against them
the feeling the need

to be a cigarette
and caress your lips
what would that be like?
a moistness somewhere inside but outside
pouting adolescent boy spoiled conceited have to kiss lips)
and we went for a walk
and it started to rain
(my favourite thing; like in a movie)
and I suggested we stand underneath this awning, you
shrugged
(your best thing, shrugging)
and then I said I'm going to embarrass you and me and
tell you something and you said go ahead and I said you
have very beautiful lips and you said, "That does not
embarrass me," and I thought what a noncommittal
answer but I pressed on wanting of course to ultimately
press against them your lips and then I stupidly brought
up that ex-wife of Hugh Hefner's, you probably don't
watch television I said, but you said that you did
(something else in common) then I told you that this
ex-wife of Hugh Hefner's (I can't remember her name)
had flesh transplanted from her buttocks to her lips and it
seemed to me that you must have had that same operation
done too, and you smoked, the cigarette caressed your
lips the cigarette taunted me "I'm touching his lips, why
don't you?" and I didn't what can I say I didn't
and later, at Rue Berri, the subway, I said bye just like
that and you seemed surprised and invited me over
to your place next maybe but you never called
so now I've written you a letter invited you to Toronto
but forever there is that moment

under the awning when you dared me
your hair so straight it was sarcastic
your eyes so dark they were imploring
your mouth your lips so full and luscious that I wanted
only to brush lightly against them
redden them press them
but I didn't
the moment came and went
and whatever happens now between us, there will never
be that particular awning, that particular rain, that
particular moment when I didn't know what you
thought, when your lips were yelling loudly but you
were saying nothing

Stop This Poem I Want to Get Off

There is a hole in this poem
It's a place for you to step in
The hole is the size of a young man
His name is Keith which I almost forgot and he didn't
call me because he got into a fight with a couple of
skinheads which probably has to do with the dreads and
the ring in his nose and of course the colour of his skin
I tried to talk to him about it
Keith likes to start political fights, which is probably why
I like him
As you can see, this poem isn't really going anywhere
But there's a place, right here
for someone (Keith? Steven? Who knows?)
To step in
O
(I know I'm a little like Shirley Jones in *The Music Man*
and this poem is my evening star, I can't help it if I'm an
operetta fan even though I like to wear cock rings but I
think you'll find, if you do a poll, that nine out of ten
operetta fans wear cock rings, at least in the privacy of
their own homes, and sometimes when they go out too.
If a boy stepped into this poem right now, he could stop
it. Go ahead, I dare you, stop my poem or I shall
continue writing on and on about nothing in the hope
that someone beautiful might stop me because that's what
writing is about really, all writers know that, it's about
having a reason not to write, it's about not having enough
time to write, it's about sneaking out of bed and going to
your computer/typewriter/pen whatever and leaving him
there sleeping and hoping that you don't wake him up
but then you do. It's about all that)

OPERETTABANQUE
(MUSIC BY LOUIS GANNE)

Those tellers are not really just clerks
I've watched them
(as they pretend to fumble with my available balance)
Nay, they are assassins, whores, robbers and slaves
That Mailene Paisan who claims to be in charge of Mutual
Funds, she's the head of it all
Clearly a dominatrix, she whips desperate, quivering
naked men with her black, lacquered hair
Luretta Moreno, of the lurid eyeshadow and the beige
lacy tops and the scarlet lips, finishes off the hapless
victims
and Little Khalam, the homely slaveboy
collects the filthy lucre
I, an unsuspecting closet case, arrive with fists clenched
to my sides, not even thinking of anal sex
Mailene lures me into her lair with vague descriptions of
ecstasy (I'm a kind of an indiscriminate masochist) and
Luretta raises the knife —
But then Johnny Muscle (robber prince disguised as a
New Accounts Manager) rushes to my side and slays
Luretta (ironically) with her own blade
Mailene tosses her porcelain frame over Luretta's inert
body (they are clearly lesbian lovers) sobbing balefully,
her hair a waterfall of regret
It is the very first time her tiny, merciless eyes have seen
their own tears
And Master Muscle carries me off, in his eponymous arms
where I learn the delights of rear entry
in his secret bandit's hideaway

It's an operetta, really
Not a bank
Which explains why they always make it so hard for me
to get at my fucking money

SEVEN SILLINESSES ABOUT
OPERA THAT REMIND ME OF YOU

1. Meeting Again and Starting Up
as if Nothing Happened

I mean I don't remember why I said goodbye to you
Yes I do you were too young I guess
And we didn't seem to have anything to say to each other
And I was very foolhardy and imagined my back
wouldn't go into spasm for three months after I said
goodbye to you
But it did
And now that I've invited you out to dinner
The possibility that we might pick up where we left off
is as silly and romantic as opera
it boggles the mind

2. Laughing to Music

Ha ha ha
They go
To the music, in time
They aren't really laughing are they
They are frivolous prostitutes who speak no dirty words
But have pretty dresses and flowers in their hair
And laugh in time to the music
Ha ha ha
That reminds me of you

3. That Moment When the Melody

That moment when the melody just disappears fades
away and they seem to be arguing with their voices,
mumbling
It's like the collective unconscious or something
They seem to have forgotten what they are singing
But it comes back
Perhaps that's what happened to us
We forgot that we were singing for a moment
The memory of the melody just disappeared
Now it's floating back
It's always there you see
It just depends on whether or not our ears are cocked
So to speak
To hear it

4. When They Sing "L'amour L'amour"

Like my old friend Christopher used to say
"Oh . . . they're just going on about love . . ."
And they do for quite a bit. At least 32 bars.
It's as if love were important and not just this construct
that we got from our parents, something to kill time with

5. He Sits Down at the Piano

He sits down at the piano and plays a tune and
suddenly everyone can sing it, perfectly in key and
harmonizing
and everyone knows the words but the words are
particularly apt
to their own particular lives and situations.
You still like to get fucked up the bum, don't you?
For hours?
Only now I know I'll have to use a condom (and pull out
too, because I do truly love you)
And you still moan the way you did?
And squirm?
And are you still just as embarrassed about having
orgasms?
I don't think so.
But that's okay.

6. They Meet at a Café

They meet at a café or party or something and fall in love
immediately even though they have nothing in common
and her murderous husband is standing over there
in the corner
singing
and he has a knife
I can't imagine what we had in common

Looking back on it now
Except that you liked to watch TV and gossip
Two of my favourite things
And you were unpretentious
And your hair was so curly
And you used to be a swimmer and your body
But I digress

7. The Heroine Is Always Fat

Always has been always will be but somehow the hero
who is a handsome young poet or painter or revolutionary
does not notice
that he can't get his arms around her
In my mind (always being the fat boy)
You might never get your arms around me
But I imagine your beautiful face
Yearning stretching trying
Your arms reaching
And you not noticing
Really not noticing
That it takes any effort at all

AN ISOLATED HOMOSEXUAL INDECENCY

It was an isolated incident like no other
a case of homosexual love
unnoticed by the press
there was no murder, killing
no suicide
there were no notes, feathers, declamatory gestures, no
makeup, couriers or discursive worriers, no falling tones,
singing queens, dying stars, lies, rejection, beer smelling,
swilling or spilling, there were no shoddy hot toddies or
party girls pressed into minutiae, pressured for an
opinion, dismissed dismayed, on display, depressed and
desiring, expiring in boas
or quotas
There was just me on the couch,
okay, I was not feeling very well
and you had just found the perfect apartment
and you came running into the room
but I was on the phone of course
gossiping with Ann
and petting the cat
and you were so filled with joy
and you looked so damn beautiful
and your skin was so white
and your fingers were so long
as they grazed your skin
moving that stray strand of hair off your young,
smiling face

that I just had to grab you
and come all over you
and then lie there late and exhausted
in the last gasp of the afternoon sun
You didn't seem to mind
If it had been printed in the papers
I would have been poised by the window, at midnight
(a creature of the dark)
in a platinum dress
a heated sheath
burning my tender skin
the gun would be smoking
you would be lying
on the floor
nasty fecal stains would have been
found
on your underwear
and discussed by the police
ad nauseum
But of course, the truth is as boring and paltry as this:
I came all over you one afternoon
because I was happy about you and your new apartment
Is it we who distort our reality, or "they"
Either way,
it's no wonder we can't seem to get
same sex spousal
benefits

(platinum dresses, your gorgeous tresses, can't seem to
find, get you out of my mind, you on the bed, confusion
in my head, transpire, perspire, the glare, heat, hair, I dare
you to care — it's me, no it's you, no it's all of us too, we
confess, we digress, it's all such a mess, but we must have
the fuss, it's so very us, the way we are, pinned on a star,
believe it or not, it's got to be hot, or else if it's not, life's
such a bore, we most fear a snore, see you later, queen!
or else in a dream — au revoir, mon petit chou,
my little cabbage,
coming all over you was fun,
love,
me)

Romantic Possibilities of the Telephone

If you think I ever went and put you on speed-dial
you are sadly mistaken
A boy has to last longer than three months
and suck my dick really well
which you didn't
Boy am I glad I put your name at the back of my
phonebook
It's EASILY erasable
there beside guys from Wisconsin and San Francisco who
I haven't called for months
and it doesn't take up too much space
(thank God!)
I might not even erase it!
The fact that you were able to find fifteen minutes
on your
fucking break
to call and break up
was not lost on me
I tried to hurry
Wouldn't want you to waste some half baked croissant
honey
and there's nothing like cold coffee
Did you put down the phone and sigh
"Oh my God he's *so* neurotic!"
to one of your co-workers
at that fucking telemarketing place?
They're all a bunch of drunks and has-beens who work
there anyways

I didn't enjoy being invited to their stupid parties
I only pretended that vulgar woman was exciting
No, telemarketers are not fascinating
contrary to your twenty-three-year-old pseudo-artistic
romanticization of them
And there's only one fucking thing I will miss
one fucking thing
and it will take a while
to get over
Turning the phone off at night
will not be easy
There is perhaps nothing sadder
after all
than a phone you expect nothing of
There it sits
still as vinegar
I guess I'll watch a late movie
And who is Betty Hutton anyway?

To the Boys of Halifax (Ode)

I didn't leave you much
just some wetness on the sheets
here and there
and a smile in a bar
and when the week was over
I was just another tired face Saturday night at RUMOURS
a gay bar
it's just like Saturday night in Toronto
horrible clones dressed all the same
shorts and shirts and sweaters
But this was To the Boys of Halifax
an ode
and especially the hairdresser 21
just a little plump beautiful hairdo, just right
he had been to TORONTO
very significant
clothes from Parachute
maybe fell a bit for me
and the two hairdressers from Newfoundland
(I always attract hairdressers)
with horrible socks on, who asked me
"Are all you guys from the university? Wow they're cute
out there, eh?"
And almost most of all for the beautiful boy from NYC
and letting me share his bed and not revealing enough
about himself so that I don't know to this day whether he
would turn out to be boring
and his skin

And the little crippled boy
who bounced around the disco
And the curly haired bartender who said
"Everybody thinks I'm a girl"
giggle
and the two tough no-nonsense dykes said
"So what's the problem, isn't that a compliment, buster?"
But most of all
and I mean this folks from the bottom of my heart
for Randy K
Who is Randy K?
I would imagine pimply, seventeen
that awkward age
dreams of Toronto
fat ugly shorts and tie-dyed shirts
freckles he's ashamed of
I don't know what he looks like
have to imagine
Randy K Halifax artist
and me at an art conference
and everybody bullshitting
about art and computers and government money
but at RUMOURS the gay disco
they have on the wall the art of Randy K
One of course is a picture of Marlene Dietrich
the other an anonymous woman's over-made-up face
but the last
I always save the best for last
THE CRYING EYE
one crying eye

and it's so badly done
that you know poor Randy K put his heart
and soul into it
and after one night after too many Old Scotians
the beer that is
and after looking in the mirror at his pimples
and after some hoser called funny little Randy K fag on
the street
for the tenth time that day
he went home and created THE CRYING EYE
one clumsy rendition of a vampy woman's eye
made up, lurid
with a long trickle of water
which turns into a limpid puddle
O Randy K you have created an image which expressed
you and Halifax and the whole lousy thing and being a
gay man which isn't easy
To the boys of Halifax
and Randy K
and the fabulous
one and only
CRYING EYE
(in the backroom by the old piano near the video machine
which is proably playing AC/DC right now as we are being
trendy and artistic here in Toronto)

LET'S REMEMBER IT, THAT AFFAIR

So she won't be able to be a fancy cabaret singer anymore
swirling about in black shiny dresses
mouthing with seeming effortlessness the voiceovers of
Marni Nixon
No, Deborah Kerr has experienced REAL tragedy
She, like so many (too many), crossed that street too fast,
without looking
(too eager, too eager aren't we all
how many a night? how many kisses
poppers up the nose
feel that thigh
oooooh he's yummy
I must have him now
oh we've all slowed down because of AIDS
that's the big lie if I've ever heard one
get me get him now not later
quick behind the wall, in the tool shed
in back of the barn under the table anywhere
down with the knickers up with the stick, quick)
Yes, we all know the indiscretion of crossing the street
without looking
So we can identify
She can no longer perform in public
But she can sit, perfectly perched in her wheelchair
subsumed, after all, with a supremely shy beauty
conducting charming impoverished children of all colours
in hymns to tomorrow, prayers for a change in fortune
chants du chance
It's a very Zen movie really
I mean we could all learn a lot from Deborah Kerr

because she doesn't expect to get Cary Grant back
anymore
no, listen, really she's content to teach music in some
back alley church school
no love, no recognition, she doesn't even TRY and get him
back
sure she buys that painting
but basically she's just letting go of the whole thing
and you can, you can do it too
Just let go of all that longing and planning and dreaming
and sit on the couch and read a book
it's Christmas and he'll come through that door
and you won't even have to do anything
you won't even have to want him
I learned a lot from Deborah Kerr, in
An Affair to Remember
And when I look at Michael, naked, in the kitchen, eating
ice cream reminding me not to be late
and perhaps, possibly, loving me (could it be?)
it seems that no matter how much I want the whole thing
to work
even though gay relationships don't last anyway
No, I am Deborah Kerr,
and I shall sit in my wheelchair
and lead orphans in song
Let the shortsighted people who don't happen to be big
Hollywood Stars
plan and get nervous
And I hear myself say, calmly
"Why I think I'll just have some of that ice cream,
Michael"

I Want to Kiss You in the Tate
(after Frank O'Hara)

But first of course, we would wander aimlessly from room
to room
blithely ignoring all museum plans
And we would discover the strawberry room
with LOVE LOCKED OUT
by Anna Lea somebody or other
I want to look at
that little boy's bum with you
as he turns away from love's door, sadly
I want to gaze for hours
at Magritte's MAN WITH NEWSPAPER
searching for a flaw
finding none
(however, there is a difference!)
I want to devour tiny Dalis
I want to faint before a Rossetti
I want to be troubled and political with you beside
a William Sickert
But most of all
(I save the best for last)
I want to stand in the middle of the room devoted to
the special Rothko exhibition
And we will know at last that there are many vast
dark doors, and we may simply gaze at them
or they may invite us in
I want to have a relationship with you that is not
imaginary
I want to have sex with you that happens again and again
only differently

I want this poem to be much less important than our love
(Just let me fuck you in the Rothko Room,
let me pull down
your pants from behind, so much for dark doors,
so I kissed
you in a Karaoke bar, so we got kicked out,
so you told me
about your dick, so you're smart, so you're hairy
so you're a lot younger than me — that's news!
— so you're a poet, so you're a poet so you're a poet so
you're a poet so you're a poet so you're a poet so you're
a poet so
you're a poet)
Okay, honey, I'll be Verlaine, if you can just get it
together to be Rimbaud!
The fantasy of course is that we will experience art
(strangulated cry!), that you will understand this poem
(moan of lust!), that I will be intimidated by your
perceptions
(oh God, I think I'm coming!),
oh the dark doors, my darling, that might await us
And when we leave the museum
Let's try not to remember
that they are only paintings

Men Are from Mars, Boys Are from Venus

GLOSSARY:
Boys: 15–30
Men: over 30

INTRODUCTION:
Boys and Men speak a different language.
When they fight, it's not so much because they are having a real disagreement, it's because they don't understand each other.
So many times, single people unknowingly turn off people they can love, and romance people they can't.
It's because they don't know the signals.
Learn new insight, new skills; get more love and support in your relationship.
These techniques have helped thousands bring love and romance back in their lives.
It's as if Boys and Men are from different planets; it's not that they don't want to be loving, it's that they don't know how.

FOR INSTANCE:
When a Boy says, "I'm not into relationships, relationships don't work,"
it really means: "I want you to fall in love with me so we can have a gay marriage that will last forever."
When a Man says, "I need more space," it means: "I need more space." (Not, "I want to break up with you," as so many Boys assume.)
When a Boy says, "Will you buy me a jacket?" it means: "Do you love me?"

When a Man says, "That hurts, don't bite me so hard," it means: "That hurts, don't bite me so hard." (Not, "Bite harder, I'm being coy!" as so many boys assume.)
When a Boy says, "I never get fucked," it means: "Fuck me now."
When a Man says, "It really doesn't matter that you don't have foreskin," it means: "It really doesn't matter that you don't have foreskin." (Not, "I desperately wish you had foreskin but I'm hiding my feelings in order not to hurt yours, because you can't help that you're Jewish.")
As a general rule, Boys mean the opposite of what they say. As a general rule, Men mean exactly what they say. Of course, the confusion comes because Men naturally expect boys to mean what they say, and Boys are always looking for hidden meanings in the sayings of Men.
As a general rule, Men like to be cuddled and nurtured. Boys like to have the living daylights fucked out of them.
And finally, remember that Men are deeply emotional beings, highly sensitive to hurt, and overly mindful of the feelings of others.
Boys have no feelings, and are cruel and shallow and evil and mean.

FINALLY:
As you can see, it's so much easier for us to live together and have rewarding relationships when we realize that:
Men are from Mars and
Boys are from Venus.

GREEN

You are green.
You tickled me.
And the funny thing was, I laughed.
As if I was green again.
There's no going back there, is there?
"And I was young and green . . ."
No, not really.
Several articles in the *New Yorker*.
A wilted flower on the desk.
A dressing gown laid carefully on the bed.
A sweet inability to come inside your ass.
Christian Slater's cheek when he was playing
a retarded boy.
I danced.
(I never dance.)
"You've got a lot of books."
Yes, I do.

Well, Kathie Lee Gifford did it.
She married some guy twenty-three years older than her.
And she's a fucking Christian.
"He's just like my dad," she says.
They had two fucking kids.
And one glorious miscarriage.
All of America loves her for it.
It's her family, after all, that got her through that
sweatshop scandal.
And God.
Don't forget about God.
Yeah, sure I forgot about God.
I forget all the time.

Yeah, you're green, you're fucking green. You don't even
know your own name. You're a goddamn acting student.
I'd have to be a goddamn teacher. I'd have to teach you
everything. And you'd do it wrong. You'd do it all
wrong. And then you'd have to do it again. And I'd
correct you. Over and over again.

Green. Fucking green.

Green #3

Like Barbara Stanwyck in *Witness To Murder*.
She saw it, she knows she fucking saw it.
There's the torn curtain.
And the earrings.
And the police say, "Lady, you just had a bad dream."
"Hey, it was no dream, and don't call me lady."
"You think you saw someone struggling."
"I don't think," she says, "I don't think, I know.
I know I saw a murder!"
She doesn't care if they think she's crazy.
She knows what she fucking saw.
Hey, Green.
I saw you.
You saw me.
Maybe you reminded me of some things.
Some things I forgot.
Like (ughgh) God.
(So somebody is going to get mad at me, some goddamn
literary critic for calling some boy God. There I go,
calling some boy God again. Fuck. God. Fuck. God.
Don't I know the difference between God and a good
fuck?)
Maybe I don't.
That's why you'd better call me green.

GREEN #4

Green, Verdi, vermilion, vert. Grass leaves weeds eyes, a
great composer dies, Il Travatore, a whore, she talks dirty,
she loves a young guy, she dies, she dies too soon, she
dies before, before she should, we pity her, she coughs,
she calls him to, to her bed, her dirty bed, her infected
bed, she says I love, I still love, cough, I'm glad I loved,
it's okay I loved, he says I, I do too, this part is ugly, it's
not pretty, the music is pretty, the blood is red, she kissed
his foot, the dirty whore, the whore is bleeding, the music
is red, the boy is green, she kissed him then, she kissed
him when, you can dress up a whore, and paint her eyes,
she's still a whore, someone pissed on the whore, she's
bleeding now, now she loves, loves the boy, boy is green,
can't go back, whore is now, bleeding red, red is green,
green knows not, red knows all, curtain is torn, earring is
found, all that's left, leave the whore, she loves you still,
for you're green, and green is good, and red is bad, except
to green, oh for god's, sake you found, found god
in, green that's okay, better to love, the green and die,
there's always blood, just don't look, know it's there,
look in his eyes, green and die.

whore love green red die god.
god green love red whore die.
die red whore love green god.
red whore love green god die.
God die! Green love red whore.

Green.

CHURCH
(FOR MICHAEL)

"Will you excuse me?
I think it's time for church.
Is it ten o'clock yet?
I should be getting to church.
Are you going to church?
I am.
I go at least once a week.
Church, I wouldn't miss it
for the world.
Everybody needs church."

So we're trying to rent out a room in our house, right,
and there's nothing but creeps come to the door, they all
seem so lonely, or have very obvious disgusting diseases,
or they don't know anything about political science, or
they don't like women, or they don't like men, or they
don't like cats, or they're one of my ex-tricks, or they're
born again non-smokers, or they have too much
furniture, or they're slum landlords in Kingston. And we
can't see why it's so difficult when our needs are simple,
when all we're looking for is an ordinary dyke slash
faggot with wit, beauty, money, a sense of style and a
neostructuralist aesthetic which though not strictly
speaking allied to Marx has a certain awareness of
Gramsci's theories of democracy, as expounded in his
prison journals?

So one afternoon a reasonably elderly faggot rings the
bell, and before he can get off his coat I realize that he's
quite drunk and soon he proves to be a very sad

character. "This is a nice room," he says, "but I know I'll never live here because you won't want me." And he gazes at me with a pitiless, frightening honesty, because of course, he's right.

And he peers at my room and at the pictures of the boys on the walls and I suddenly wish I hadn't worn my tightest pants and then we have to make chat with him which is torture until a half an hour or so passes and there are so many pauses in the conversation that he gets the idea, and staggers towards the door.

Not without a parting word, though. He struggles to his full five foot eight inches wiggles his finger at me and intones "See you in church!"

And I ask Bob and Sue what that means and they say, "It's a gay expression." Gay expression? I just love gay expressions.

But what does it mean? "Oh," say Bob and Sue, "it clearly means see you at the bars or the baths or — wherever."

Well I never heard that before,

See you in church.

But I do remember being a little boy in church. And even though it made me nervous and I used to get anxiety attacks I also remember beautiful moments in church, sitting in the pews and getting tingles down my spine and thinking about God.

It's nice to imagine I got the tingles because of God but I think it was because of the church music.

I just loved it, the organ and the choir and my own quivering voice — noble thrilling enthralling inspiring shiver.

And then I think about gay bars and how they're a little like church.

No they are, they've got the music, too, and they are like temples, vast temples with swirling lights and thundering music and worship and what do they worship? The male body. And some of you may not think that's worth worshipping but I do, and then I think about Michael, my latest, who appears at my house in the cutest little blue cap and just jerking off for hours and watching him come and his beautiful white body and it's night and he opens the curtains so that we can see ourselves and the moon and his fine young muscles and his smooth hardness pressed against mine.
Oh boy yes, boy yes give in let go come for me, come.

And that's what I wanted to say to you people, that I'm a really religious person, I am.

Oh yeah, one more thing —

"See you in church."

LIGHTER THAN AIR

When people ask me what I see in younger men I always
think of walking
past Christ Church in Montreal
before it was the mall
"Under construction"
people used to stop and stare
They dug out the basement of the church and it seemed
suspended it seemed
to be flying the buttresses like wings the cool dry
underbelly brightly lit by work
lights — what happens underneath the church? What goes
on? What supports it? What are those men doing
underneath that church?
Those were the days when Christ Church Montreal
floated above St. Catherine's Street and the passersby
stopped to stare, wondering why it was suddenly lighter
than air
Recently I walked by Christ Church
The construction is completed
The cool bright underbelly has been encased in concrete
No one really looks at the new church now
"It's an architectural marvel," they say,
"a church with a mall underneath"
and walk away without blinking
And I think of Dennis, 22, clear bright eyes, a shock of
hair that reaches down to his chin "I have to get it cut"
and when I painted a picture for him it was "the best
present I ever got" and Dennis is the best present I ever
got because he is perched absolutely expectant, only the
best ahead, absolutely romantic and I've never seen his
large full cock when it wasn't erect

It is, I suppose, callous of me to want Dennis now instead
of 20 years from now when people will walk by him
without blinking and when his yearning will be encased
in concrete
I want my men under construction, lighter than air and I
can still wonder what holds them up, with their cocks
arched like flying buttresses and their eyelashes fluttering
like wings

Peter had invited me for coffee, first,
at that restaurant with the unpronounceable name
and of course he was sitting there with James.
I was impressed, as well I should be.
(Isn't it interesting the way people introduce the ones
they love? "Sky this is James," and of course, I tripped
and almost fell into him and then he wanted to know
about my tattoo. It's important not to be too fascinating
— result: jealousy, or too disinterested — result: hurt)
James asked about the various forms of neuroses and
Peter was in his element — father, teacher, pedant, wit:
"Well Gestalt describes three types of neurosis:
projection, introjection and retrogression."
Peter and I agree that we have all three. James is confused
and interested, and goes home, almost stealing Peter's hat.
As Peter and I make our trek to the strip bar I realize that
the poets are wrong; one-sided love is not hopeless — it's
the other way around. Peter and James are clearly in love
with each other equally, and that of course is why they
will never be happy together. The obsession is *too* equal.
Neither is crying and sighing hopelessly. Neither is
telling the other what to do (I.E.: MARRIAGE). Two
people equally in love? That's a stalemate, a prison, two
pairs of eyes endlessly staring fearfully into the void.
Dare I know that soul (it loves me as I love it)? Why no,
I dare not.
And we're at the strip bar and the boys whirl perilously
around us. One boy has made pants out of ripped jeans
and a pair of chaps. Another surprises us with his long
cock. Another sits, pouting, by the slot machine, but
every time he moves, Peter and I gasp.

And of course these boys make me think about death. As they always do.

For those who are obsessed with the body are obsessed with death. We are all too aware of how the body changes. Each pimple, each wrinkle, announces death's imminence.

And you can lock yourself in your house and roll up your windows and make dinner.

Or you can throw yourself into the body of that young man, with every ounce of fury you have left.

Death will come either way. But we imagine that watching its inevitable approach is a kind of cheat, is beating the game.

And we are always running, with our back to the moon, and hiding, with our face in the sun, and yelling, with the music in our ears.

Our desperate escapes! How we love them, as we love our boys, and though we are reluctant to admit it, they love us too.

Or then again, perhaps we're just two old queens sipping beer at the Adonis, and it needn't be any more important than that.

A Poem for Maria Delmonte

1. Gazing at Glenn Gould. There is some horrible man talking to him. A producer. The producer is standing up. "What did you think of it that time?" "Very macho," says Glenn, with a pianistic gesture. "Next time it will have to be without the vocal obligato," says the sucky producer. Glenn Gould looks up from his squatting position on the floor. And I realize: He is the James Dean of the piano. It's not just that he was extra good, you see, or a genius, or whatever. It's just . . . well to play the Italian Concerto with such authority. And then to look like that, after. That's something special.

2. I'm standing at the 501 alone watching a drag queen. She's very good. Her name is Maria Delmonte (named after those special fruits). She sings completely in Spanish. None of us white boys know what she's singing. Onstage, she is very beautiful. Offstage, she would be a short boy with a hook nose. Onstage she is weaving Spanish spells of mystery, romance, guitars, bad, funny sex. We love her. Again, we have no idea what she is saying. I think it's because she's so pretty and so talented. Or at least she made us think she was.

3. I'm trying to figure out a way to say Good-bye, finally, in a poem or writing or something. Why not here. And it seems to me that you were both Glenn Gould and Maria Delmonte. All that potential. All that beauty. It's too bad I had to end up hating you. That's all I have to say really. I had this Shakespearean Sonnet fantasy that your inside matched your outside. I was wrong.

4. Yesterday I was eating lunch at the University and this fantastically attractive boy sat down beside me, all fuzzy blonde hair and muscles. He started to eat his spaghetti and then he opened an anatomy book. (Of course, possessed of that commanding brow and that disdain, he could only be a medical student.) Not thinking of me (and why should he?) he laid the anatomy book down on the table. There were horrible pictures of runny human innards; it ruined my Shepherd's Pie. "How can you eat your lunch and read that book?" I asked. He looked up at me, surprised. "Oh, you get used to it after a while," he said.

5. I have one final question.

Do you?

Thoughts on "Bringing Up Baby"

It was a sad Sunday
And I didn't like it at first
I was all prepared to be cranky about Howard Hawks
I mean let's face it
It's all a setup really
Katharine Hepburn's little voice is very annoying and fake
And Cary Grant's coke bottle glasses are so obvious
It wasn't delightful at all, to me
As I struggled awake through Saturday night's hangover
and memories of bad sex
the night before
And then somewhere, I think it was when I realized
she was carrying a butterfly net to catch a leopard
yes, it was there, I think
that I realized that this movie had absolutely nothing to
do with reality
and that's what made it so fabulous
So I was gone
And when they're singing
"I can't give you anything but love, baby"
to the leopard outside the psychiatrist's window
and the leopard is howling along, and so is the dog
and the psychiatrist's wife says to Katharine Hepburn
with the condescension of the sane:
"You just keep on singing, dear"
and Katharine Hepburn doesn't miss a beat when she says
"Oh, I will!"
And that is, of course, what we all have to do, in the
midst of all the insanity and death
(sorry, I didn't mean to mention death)

we have to keep on singing
And before long, everyone is in jail, and no one knows
their names anymore,
and Katharine Hepburn is acting butch, and this is what
we've been waiting for, the whole movie, for her to drop
that plummy accent and the femmy gestures and just get
down to business
And the point isn't merely that the insane are more sane
or that power structures must be toppled (hence the
dinosaur skeleton falling at the end)
no it's that there, within insanity lies truth, beauty
Yes beauty
Or else why would I have been at the baths the other
night
with a boy I love
watching him screw other people?
I can't explain why I love him
It's like when David says he just has to get
fucked up the bum
or else he thinks the guy doesn't really love him
It's like when Pasolini explains that he is obsessed with
boys
because their body hair keeps on growing until they're
twenty-five
One tries to categorize and organize one's love, one's
desire
And then one realizes that one is using a butterfly net to
catch a leopard
isn't one?
For there is a certain blessedness in being hysterical
Forgetting who we are is perhaps the only answer
And for certain we will find out if there's a "good
leopard"

or a "bad leopard"
at the end of that rope
It will either tear us to pieces or purr
But as Katharine Hepburn reminds us
at the end of the movie
all the time we were merely searching for a good bone
a good hard clean bone that might finish off that dinosaur
skeleton
Watch out!
The skeleton is shaking . . .
But oh, what a fall

THE ISLAND OF LOST TEARS

Haven't you heard the latest news about AIDS?
You can get it from tears
O yes
You mustn't let anyone cry on you or
cry near you, in fact it's a very good idea not to let
anyone cry in the same room as you
We have received notice that at the moment authorities
are considering taking all the weepers (all the wettest
people in the world) — shipping them off, and putting
them on a small island off Southern England where they
can all weep on each other to their heart's content and it
rains there all the time anyway so they won't know the
difference
And all those great movies
the tearjerkers:
*The Heiress, Now Voyager, Madame X, Love Is a Many
Splendored Thing, The Rainmaker, The Rains of
Ranchipur* and even for you really sappy ones, parts of
The Music Man
will no longer be allowed on TV
And if you know someone who's a sentimental type
you'd better warn them, you'd better have a heart to
heart or safer yet, a mind to mind, and say, "In the past
you were wont to get emotional at the slightest
provocation. Though there's nothing really wrong with
being emotional — everyone, in the past, got emotional
from time to time — now, because of what we know
about tears, it's better that you try to control yourself
and not get into situations where you might be moved.

You know . . . one thing leads to another and just taking casual notice of an impoverished beggar woman or watching a sunset for an extended length of time, for many, could lead to such minor yet dangerous feelings as sadness, love, pity, affection, and from these it is but a short step to the dreaded tears. For some even the old fashioned notion of warmth will become a thing of the past. Certainly old habits die hard, many will be unwilling to give up their emotional lives. But the danger to human health is too great. Do yourself a favour. Stop feeling deeply. Your partner, your lover, your husband wife or significant other will thank you for your consideration in repressing your deepest most profound emotions."

But me
I will go
To the Island of Lost Tears
No boat will take you there
No plane will fly you there
You must find your own way
Some swim, some walk on the water
Some claim they fly there
and as you approach
you can hear the faint sounds of sobbing
and you see nothing
but a lush greenery shrouded in mist
And when you reach the shore
they rush to you
and hold you
in their strong arms
arms made so much stronger warmer by being caressed
with tears

And they take you to their
wet little houses
and sit you down by their
wet little fires
and they say to you
"Cry
my sweet boy
my inscrutable girl
cry until you have no more tears
until the very well that is your sadness and your joy is dry
and when you think that you can cry no more
you find that you can cry still!"
No one dies there
in the Island of Lost Tears
they simply fade into the mist
But late at night through the trees
(they have none but weeping willows)
the voices whisper the forbidden words
"Weep . . . cry . . . feel . . . let yourself go!"
These are the ghosts of those who dared
to cry when all others had forgotten how, and they will
not be silent.

Writer, filmmaker, actor, or drag queen extraordinaire . . .
Sky Gilbert is one of North America's most controversial
artistic forces. He was born in Norwich, Connecticut, but
since 1965, Toronto has been his home. The co-founder
of Toronto's Buddies in Bad Times Theatre, for two
decades Gilbert has written and directed his own hit
plays, including *The Dressing Gown* and *Capote at
Yaddo*. In 1985 he received the Pauline McGibbon Award
for directing, and he has also received two prestigious
Dora Mavor Moore Awards. Gilbert's third film, *My
Summer Vacation*, was featured at the San Francisco
International Lesbian and Gay Film Festival. His first
novel, *Guilty*, was published in 1998 by Insomniac Press.
Digressions of a Naked Party Girl is his first full-length
collection of poetry.